STANDARD BOOK OF

GUCCI

Dive into the Heart of Luxury and Innovation

Chloé Kamali-Worth

STANDARD BOOK OF

GUCCI

1921

CHLOE KAMALI-WORTH

uccio Gucci, founder of one of the most prestigious fashion houses in the world, as left his mark on the luxury sector with his innate sense of style and elegance. orn in 1881 in Florence, Italy, Guccio began his career in the hotel industry, which lowed him to travel Europe and be inspired by the sophistication and ophistication he observed, particularly in Paris and London. These experiences id the foundation for what would become a brand synonymous with luxury, uality and innovation in fashion. In 1921, he returned to his hometown of orence to open his first boutique, specializing in high-quality leather goods, veraging local artisanal know-how to create products that embodied Italian egance.

nder Guccio's leadership, Gucci expanded rapidly, becoming famous for its andcrafted leather bags, shoes and travel items, which catered to a wealthy ientele, including celebrities and members of the royal family. His attention to etail, commitment to quality and innovative use of leather, such as calfskin, xotic leather and bamboo, have set high standards in the fashion industry. After s death in 1953, his sons took over and continued to develop the brand ternationally, while remaining true to their father's legacy. Today, Gucci is a obal symbol of fashion and luxury, carrying forward the spirit of innovation and

The codes of luxury
Gucci

The codes of Gucci luxury embody a unique fusion of Italian tradition, innovation and a touch of eccentricity, reflecting the evolution of the brand since its creation by Guccio Gucci in 1921. Under the direction of several artistic directors, Gucci has managed to preserve its legacy while continuing to reinvent itself. Here are some of the key elements that define the codes of luxury at Gucci:

1. **Italian Craftsmanship:** At the heart of Gucci's identity is an unwavering commitment to high-quality craftsmanship. Traditional leather crafting techniques, attention to detail and the use of premium materials are the cornerstones of the brand, reflecting its rich Italian heritage.
2. **Iconic motifs:** Gucci is famous for its distinctive motifs and logos, such as the double G, green and red stripes and the Diamante motif. These elements have become synonymous with the brand, providing instant recognition and continuity between collections.
3. **Eclecticism and innovation:** Gucci stands out for its bold approach to design, mixing historical, cultural and contemporary references. Under the direction of Alessandro Michele, the brand has adopted a maximalist aesthetic, characterized by mixes of patterns, bright colors and attention to ornate details.
4. **Commitment to Sustainability:** Gucci is increasingly committed to sustainable practices, with the aim of reducing its environmental impact and promoting responsible fashion. This pivot towards sustainability highlights a new dimension of luxury, combining aesthetics and environmental responsibility.
5. **Collaborations and capsule collections:** Gucci has embraced collaborations with artists, designers and brands from diverse backgrounds, creating unique capsule collections that blend Gucci's DNA with external influences, illustrating its spirit of openness and innovation.
6. **Storytelling:** Each Gucci collection tells a story, weaving together themes, motifs and references that enrich the brand experience. This narrative approach adds a layer of depth to his creations, inviting consumers to be part of a universe larger than the product itself.

01

Founded by Guccio Gucci: Gucci was founded in 1921 in Florence, Italy, by Guccio Gucci, initially as a boutique selling handcrafted luxury leather goods.

02

Equestrian inspiration: Gucci's early designs were heavily inspired by the equestrian world, hence the use of motifs such as the horsebit and the green-red-green Web stripe which have become iconic for the brand.

Equestrian models

Equestrian motifs from Gucci

- **The horse's bit:** This element, part of the horse's harness, has been stylized and used in many Gucci products, including bags, shoes and belts. The horse bit symbolizes Gucci's connection to equestrianism and has been interpreted in various ways over the years, becoming one of the brand's most recognizable motifs.

- **The green-red-green Web ribbon:** While the Web ribbon is now synonymous with Gucci, it also has its origins in the equestrian world. Inspired by straps used in horse riding, the green-red-green web stripe was introduced in the 1950s. Originally it represented a symbol of excellence and luxury. Over time it has become a distinctive element of Gucci, symbolizing the brand's identity and its heritage.

Equestrian influence on the design

The equestrian inspiration goes beyond the patterns and also influences the product design. For example, bags often feature clasps and details reminiscent of equestrian tack, and clothing can include elements such as blazers and trousers inspired by traditional equestrian attire.

Evolution and modernity

Under the guidance of various creative designers over the years, Gucci has successfully reinterpreted its equestrian heritage in a modern and fashionable way. Traditional equestrian motifs have been given a contemporary twist, proving that historical inspiration can blend with modernity to create something unique and recognisable.

03

Ryan Gosling, **the Canadian actor known for his roles in films such as "La La Land" and "Drive," has also been associated with Gucci, known for its collaborations with high-profile celebrities and influencers. This collaboration between Gosling and Gucci is part of the fashion house's tradition of collaborating with personalities from the world of cinema, music and art to embody the spirit of the brand, both in its advertising campaigns and during haute couture events.**

04

Material Innovation: During World War II, Gucci innovated by using bamboo for bag handles due to restrictions on traditional materials, creating the famous Bamboo bag.

A *material revolution in wartime*

Innovation in the use of materials has always been at the heart of Gucci's philosophy, and one of the most notable examples of this approach is the creation of the famous Bamboo bag during World War II. At that time, Italy, like many other countries, faced severe restrictions on traditional materials due to the needs of the war effort. This has forced fashion houses to get creative with available resources.

Guccio Gucci then had the revolutionary idea of using bamboo, an abundant but until then little used material in European luxury, for the handles of his bags. Not only was bamboo available, but it also provided the ideal strength and flexibility to be shaped into elegant, durable handles. Gucci artisans heated bamboo sticks and then bent them by hand to create this iconic and distinctive shape.

Once launched, Gucci's Bamboo bag quickly became a symbol of innovation and elegance, worn by celebrities and style figures around the world. Its unique design and its ingenious genesis not only demonstrated Gucci's ability to innovate in the face of adversity, but also established the brand as a leader in the use of unconventional materials in haute couture.

Today, the Bamboo bag remains one of Gucci's most iconic designs, a testament to the ingenuity and creative flair that continues to define the brand.

GUCCI BAMBOO 1947 MEDIUM HANDBAG

05

International Expansion: In the 1950s,
Gucci began to expand internationally, opening
boutiques in New York, London, Paris, and
Tokyo, becoming a global luxury brand.

Gucci international

Gucci's international expansion in the 1950s ushered in a new era for the brand, transforming it from a local success to a global fashion powerhouse.

This strategy of opening stores in key cities such as New York, London, Paris and Tokyo not only allowed Gucci to capture an affluent international clientele but also helped forge its cosmopolitan identity.

Gucci's presence in these fashion capitals has facilitated collaborations with celebrities and influential style figures, amplifying its status as a symbol of luxury and elegance around the world.

This expansion laid the foundation for what Gucci is today: a truly global brand, whose influence crosses borders and cultures, while remaining rooted in its rich Italian heritage.

06

Iconic symbols: The double G logo, introduced in the 1960s, has become a global symbol of luxury and style, representing the initials of Guccio Gucci. Its elegant design and ability to embody both the brand's tradition and innovation have cemented its place as a true status icon, spanning generations to become a staple for fashion enthusiasts around the world.

Iconic symbols

Gucci's double G logo, one of the brand's most iconic visual signatures, represents much more than just a brand. Introduced in the 1960s, this model quickly became synonymous with luxury, elegance and distinctive style, embodying the spirit of the Italian fashion house founded by Guccio Gucci.

This logo is composed of two stylized letters "G", intertwined to form a unique pattern, recognizable among all. The upside-down "G" pays homage to Guccio Gucci, the founder, and highlights the family legacy at the heart of the brand's identity. The creation of this logo coincides with a period of strong international expansion for Gucci, helping the brand establish a consistent and powerful visual presence in global markets.

Beyond its aesthetic appearance, the double G logo symbolizes the fusion of traditional sophistication and modern innovation that characterizes Gucci. It represents excellence in craftsmanship, quality of materials and meticulous attention to detail, values that Guccio Gucci has instilled from the beginning. Over the decades, this logo has adorned a multitude of products, from bags and accessories to clothing and shoes, becoming a sign of recognition and guarantee of prestige for those who wear them.

The timelessness and versatility of the double G logo has allowed Gucci to reinterpret it across different eras and trends, without ever losing its essence. Whether subtly etched into skin or displayed more ostentatiously on ready-to-wear pieces, the double G logo remains a pillar of Gucci's visual identity, a symbol immediately associated with luxury and innovation in the world of fashion.

07

Diversification: In addition to leather goods, Gucci has diversified into apparel, shoes, watches, jewelry, accessories, fragrances and home decor, becoming a comprehensive fashion and lifestyle brand.

INSPIRATIONAL FASHION OUTFIT OF THE DAY

CHOOSE AN
ELEGANT GUCCI
LOOK

everyday

08

Changes in creative direction: Gucci has seen several influential artistic directors at the helm, including Tom Ford in the 1990s and early 2000s, who revitalized the brand with his sexy, modern aesthetic, and more recently Alessandro Michele, known for his eclectic and romantic approach.

09

Tom Ford L.A. - Autumn/Winter 2020 - Women's collection - New York - © PixelFormula

Tom Ford radically transformed Gucci in the 1990s from a struggling brand to a fashion titan, most notably with his Autumn/Winter 1995 collection which presented a bold and sensual vision, marking the beginning of a new era for Gucci.

10

Tom Ford L.A. - Autumn/Winter 2020 - Men's collection - New York - © PixelFormula

As president of the CFDA and an accomplished director with works such as **"A Single Man" and "Nocturnal Animals,"** Tom Ford blends fashion and film, his designs being staples of Hollywood red carpets.

When Tom Ford captures Hollywood and reinvents Gucci

The front row shone under the spotlight, captivated by the presence of celebrities such as Miley Cyrus, Jennifer Lopez and Renée Zellweger. Tom Ford's latest collection, which mixes men's and women's ready-to-wear, stands out for the use of luxurious and sensual materials, such as black lace and satin, chosen in rich, deep shades.

Clean designs prevailed, punctuated here and there by floral motifs or animal prints. The outfits, with a free and relaxed look, seemed to draw inspiration from the crucial period between the end of the 60s and the beginning of the 70s, perhaps deliberately recalling the atmosphere of the film "Once Upon a Time in Hollywood" by Quentin Tarantino .

The latter, set in the summer of 1969, is among the main contenders at this Sunday's Academy Awards, with the possibility of Brad Pitt winning his first Oscar. Renée Zellweger is also up for an award, praising her performance as Judy Garland in the film "Judy."

TOM FORD

SPRING-SUMMER 2023

11

Commitment to Sustainability: Gucci is committed to sustainability with its Gucci Equilibrium initiative, aimed at reducing its environmental impact and promoting diversity and inclusion.

12

Role in pop culture: Gucci has been immortalized in numerous songs, films and television series, becoming synonymous with wealth, style and exclusivity in global popular culture.

GUCCI   SAINT LAURENT   BOTTEGA VENETA

BALENCIAGA   Alexander McQUEEN   Brioni
ROMA

BOUCHERON   Pomellato   qeelin
PARIS

ULYSSE NARDIN   GIRARD-PERREGAUX
SINCE 1846   LE LOCLE · SUISSE

KERING
EYEWEAR

13

Acquisition by Kering: In 1999, Gucci became part of the French luxury group Kering (formerly PPR), joining other renowned luxury brands.

14

Digital Initiatives: Gucci was one of the first luxury brands to embrace e-commerce and social media, establishing a strong and interactive online presence that reflects its innovative brand image.

Gucci and digital: pioneers of innovation in luxury

Gucci, a pioneer in the world of luxury, quickly grasped the crucial importance of digital to remain at the forefront of innovation and the market. By embracing e-commerce and investing heavily in social media, Gucci has not only expanded its reach but also strengthened its image as a cutting-edge brand. This strategic approach has enabled the brand to forge closer ties with its customers around the world, offering a seamless online shopping experience and engaging in direct conversations with consumers via social platforms.

Gucci's early integration of digital technologies reflects its desire to break the traditional boundaries of fashion, making its collections accessible to a wider audience and creating personalized experiences for customers. Gucci's digital initiatives, from innovative mobile apps to interactive social media advertising campaigns, have not only increased the brand's visibility, but have also set new standards in the luxury industry for online engagement and digital creativity.

Gucci's early and successful adoption of digital has played a key role in its contemporary success, demonstrating that digital innovation can coexist harmoniously with traditional luxury to create a dynamic, accessible and thoroughly modern brand.

15

Gucci
Garden

ARCHETYPES

GUCCI
Garden
SYDNEY

Gucci Garden: In Florence, the Gucci Garden is a unique space that combines a museum, a boutique and a restaurant, offering an immersion in the aesthetics and philosophy of the brand.

The Gucci Garden

The Gucci Garden, nestled in the heart of Florence in the historic Palazzo della Mercanzia, is an unmissable destination for admirers of the brand and fashion enthusiasts from around the world. More than just a museum, the Gucci Garden is a living celebration of the creativity and innovative spirit that has characterized Gucci since its creation. Designed under the creative vision of Alessandro Michele, the brand's artistic director, this one-of-a-kind space offers total immersion in the world of Gucci, combining history, art and fashion.

Through the different rooms of the Palace, visitors are invited to explore the evolution of Gucci, from its beginnings in 1921 to its current status as a global fashion giant. Regularly updated exhibitions feature rare archive pieces, contemporary art installations and iconic brand creations, illustrating the constant dialogue between past and present that drives Gucci. Each room is conceived as a living painting, where clothes, accessories, works of art and decorative elements interact to tell the story of the Florentine house.

The Gucci Garden is also home to the Gucci Osteria boutique, a gourmet restaurant run by the famous Michelin three-star chef Massimo Bottura. The Osteria offers innovative cuisine that, like Michele's creations, pushes the boundaries of tradition to offer a unique culinary experience. Diners can enjoy dishes inspired by Bottura's travels and love of contemporary art, in an environment that reflects Gucci's eclectic aesthetic.

Gucci Garden features a boutique offering exclusive items, one-of-a-kind pieces and special collaborations, available only on site. This offers visitors the opportunity to take home a piece of the Gucci universe, from fashion and accessories to stationery and home furnishings.

16

Fight against counterfeiting: Gucci is actively engaged in the fight against counterfeiting, protecting its designs and assets through legal action and awareness campaigns.

17

Diversity and inclusion: Under the leadership of Alessandro Michele, Gucci has emphasized diversity and inclusion, both in its advertising campaigns and in its modeling choices, reflecting a more open and diverse society.

Alessandro Michele

18

Gucci Osteria: The brand has also extended its influence into the world of gastronomy, with the opening of several Gucci Osteria restaurants by Michelin-starred chef Massimo Bottura, in Italy, the United States and elsewhere.

Andrew Moncrief exhibition, Gucci, 161, boulevard Saint-Germain, Paris, during men's fashion week.

19

Supporting artists and creators: Gucci has launched several initiatives to support young artists and creators around the world, highlighting its commitment to creativity and innovation across all industries.

20

Commitment to mental health: The brand has made significant commitments to mental health, particularly through awareness campaigns and support for organizations working in this sector, thus demonstrating its social involvement beyond fashion.

21

Gucci Changemakers: Launched in 2019, the Gucci Changemakers program aims to support diversity and inclusion within the creative community and beyond. This investment fund focuses on funding scholarships and grants for non-profit organizations that promote equal opportunities in the fashion and creative industries.

PREVIEW

[ACCESSORY]

Gucci accessories, symbols of elegance and refinement, perfectly embody the essence of Italian luxury.

From belts adorned with the famous GG logo to bold and innovative sunglasses, each piece reflects a harmonious marriage of traditional craftsmanship and modern aesthetics. Silk scarves, infused with colorful patterns and iconic designs, add a touch of sophistication to any outfit, while Gucci watches combine functionality and high-fashion design, demonstrating the brand's meticulous attention to detail.

TRENDS PROJECTS
COLLECTIONS FACES
DESIGNERS AWARDS

Bags, from the classic Bamboo and Dionysus to the recent Marmont models, have become objects of desire all over the world, symbols of status and style. Constantly innovating while preserving its heritage, Gucci continues to redefine luxury accessories, elevating them to wearable works of art that captivate and inspire.

ITALY🌐

22

The Gucci ArtLab: in Florence, the Gucci ArtLab is an innovation center dedicated to the experimentation and creation of leather and ready-to-wear products, symbolizing the brand's commitment to craftsmanship, innovation and sustainability .

23

Impact on Fashion Shows: Gucci fashion shows are known for their theatricality and innovation, often featuring intricate narratives and settings that transform the presentation of fashion into an immersive art form.

24

Collaborations with artists and brands: Gucci has collaborated with an eclectic range of artists, designers and brands from diverse fields, ranging from fashion to art to lifestyle, creating unique pieces that blend the Gucci aesthetic with various cultural influences .

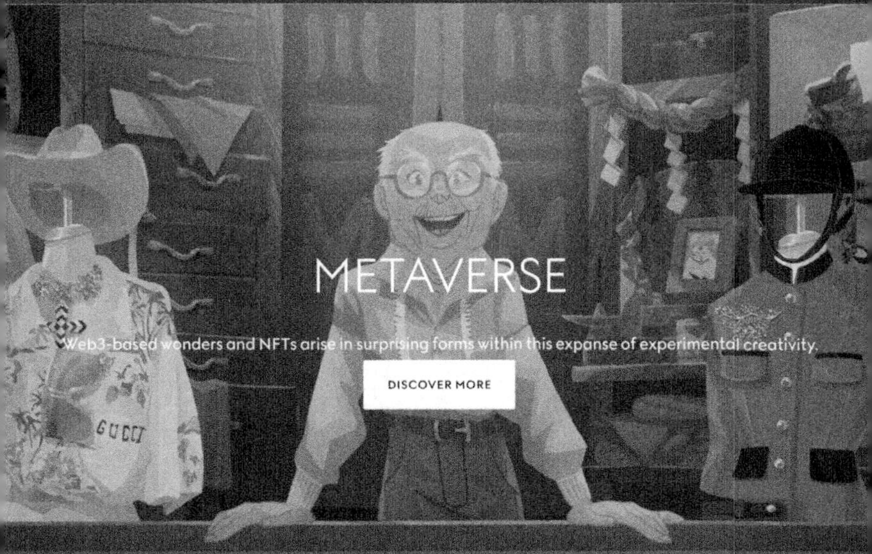

METAVERSE

Web3-based wonders and NFTs arise in surprising forms within this expanse of experimental creativity.

DISCOVER MORE

25

Gucci Vault: Launching in 2021, Gucci Vault is an experiential online platform designed as a space to explore vintage collaborations, rare pieces and exclusive capsule collections, reflecting the brand's avant-garde spirit.

26

Participation in circular fashion initiatives:
Gucci is committed to the circular fashion
movement, launching resale and recycling
programs to extend the life of its products and
reduce environmental impact.

27

Global influence on fashion: Gucci continues to influence global fashion trends, not only through its collections but also through its cultural, social and environmental approach, establishing its role as a leader in the luxury sector.

28

Influence in gaming: Gucci has embraced the world of video games by collaborating with games such as "The Sims" and "Pokémon GO", offering an immersive brand experience in the digital world and thus reaching a younger and more tech-savvy audience.

29

The Gucci for Women program: Launched to support female entrepreneurship, this program demonstrates Gucci's commitment to promoting gender equality and supporting women leaders across various industries.

THE
Guccio Gucci
MODIFIES IT

stylist

G Uccio Gucci, the founder of one of the world's most iconic luxury brands, laid the foundation for a fashion empire that transcends generations Born in 1881 in Florence, Italy, Guccio began his journey into the world of luxury by opening the his first boutique in Florence 1921,

The history of Gucci is not limited to its founder; extends to his family, who have played a crucial role in the expansion and success of the brand. His sons, Aldo, Vasco, Ugo and Rodolfo, inherited their father's entrepreneurial spirit, each contributing to Gucci's international expansion in the 1950s and 1960s. Under their leadership, Gucci established itself as a symbol of luxury, opening boutiques in New York. London and Paris, and introduced iconic products that have become synonymous with the brand, such as the Bamboo bag and horsebit loafers.

The Gucci dynasty: a saga at the heart of luxury

The story of the Gucci family is an epic tale full of twists and turns, embodying both the triumph and tragedies of a dynasty that has had a profound impact on the world of luxury fashion. Founded in 1921 by Guccio Gucci in Florence, the house of Gucci began as a modest leather goods boutique before rising to the rank of one of the biggest names in global luxury. This spectacular rise is the result of a mix of innovation, passion and, of course, family drama.

The First Steps of a Legend Guccio Gucci, inspired by the elegance and sophistication he had observed during his travels to Paris and London, opened his first boutique focusing on quality craftsmanship and sophisticated design. His sons, Aldo, Vasco, Ugo and Rodolfo, joined the company, contributing to its international expansion in the 1950s and 1960s, particularly in New York, where Gucci became synonymous with luxury and sophistication.

Success and family disagreements With success, however, also came tensions. Arguments over the management of the company tore the family apart, especially between Aldo Gucci and his son Paolo, the latter later revealing tax problems that led to Aldo's conviction. These internal power struggles eventually led to the company being sold to an outside investor in the 1990s, marking the end of the Gucci family's direct involvement in the brand.

The legacy and influence continues

Despite the conflicts, the Gucci family legacy remains undeniable. The brand continues to thrive, building on the foundations laid by Guccio and his sons to push the boundaries of fashion and innovation. Iconic creative directors like Tom Ford and Alessandro Michele have drawn from the brand's rich history to create collections that pay homage to its legacy while projecting it into the future.

Beyond fashion: a cultural symbol

The saga of the Gucci family has captured the public imagination far beyond the fashion industry, with stories of its rise and internal struggles adapted for films and books, highlighting the family's lasting impact on popular culture and the world of luxury.

The history of the Gucci family is characterized by a spectacular rise, marked by innovation and family drama. Their legacy continues to influence the brand today, reminding us that behind every Gucci creation is a story of passion, power and undeniable beauty.

30

Educational initiatives: Gucci is engaged in educational projects, including the Gucci Education Program, which aims to provide resources and training in the field of fashion and design for young emerging talents.

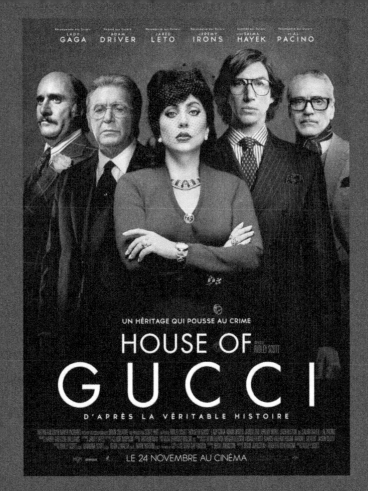

31

Film Premieres: Gucci has often sponsored film premieres and collaborated with the film industry, underlining its close connection to the world of cinema and its ability to influence and be influenced by pop culture.

"House of Gucci": Immerse yourself in a fashion dynasty between luxury and scandals

The film "House of Gucci", inspired by dramatic events that actually happened, immerses us in the turmoil that marked the history of the famous Gucci fashion house. This gripping and tragic saga explores the controversial takeover of the brand and the sensational murder of Maurizio Gucci, providing a fascinating insight into an important part of fashion history.

Despite the fictionalized nature of the biopic and some liberties taken with actual facts - as highlighted by Gucci family members themselves - "House of Gucci" offers a fascinating look at the origins and evolution of one of the world's most iconic fashion houses , the world. Adapted from the book "The Gucci Saga" by Sara Gay Forden, the film has sparked debate over its faithfulness to historical events and casting choices, which some say do not do justice to the true protagonists of the story.

The film returns to Gucci's origins, portraying Guccio Gucci, its founder, as a visionary who honed his taste for luxury during his time in London. Returning to Italy, he opened his first luggage shop in 1921, innovating through the use of alternative materials such as hemp, linen and bamboo, thus laying the foundations of a family empire destined to shine on the international scene.

"House of Gucci" does not stop there and also explores one of the most transformative periods of the brand with the arrival of Tom Ford as CEO.

creative in 1994. Ford, with his bold and sensual aesthetic, projected Gucci into the era of "porno-chic" glamour, marking an important stylistic break with the traditional vision of the founders. The film captures this watershed moment with the Spring/Summer 1997 collection show, in which provocative dresses and high cuts reinvented Gucci's image, ushering the brand into a new era of sensuality and commercial success.

Beyond the fashion-centric plot, "House of Gucci" is a reflection on ambition, power and family, weaving a story full of emotions and twists. Despite the controversy surrounding its making, the film remains a captivating work for anyone interested in the history of fashion, the evolution of luxury empires and the complexity of the family dynasties behind major brands.

32

Restoration of cultural heritage: Gucci has participated in the restoration of historical monuments and works of art, including the famous Boboli Gardens in Florence, illustrating its commitment to the preservation of art and culture.

33

The restoration of the famous Boboli Gardens in Florence. This project illustrates the importance that the brand attributes to art and culture, recognizing their role in safeguarding history and the environment. By investing in the restoration of this historic garden, Gucci not only contributes to the beautification of the space, but also helps to keep an important Italian cultural heritage alive for future generations, strengthening the link between fashion, art and durability.

34

Impact on fashion trends: Gucci collections have often anticipated or defined fashion trends, with pieces and looks that have been widely adopted by consumers and celebrated by fashion critics.

35

Commitment to LGBTQ+ Rights: Gucci has expressed its support for the LGBTQ+ community through campaigns, special collections and partnerships with organizations dedicated to promoting equality and inclusion.

Gucci and the LGBT+ *community*

Gucci, as a luxury giant, has always been at the forefront of fashion, but its commitment to the LGBT+ community demonstrates that the brand is also at the forefront of social change and inclusion. Through bold initiatives and collaborations with public figures, Gucci demonstrates that luxury can rhyme with activism, making fashion a vector of visibility and support for LGBT+ rights.

Collections that celebrate diversity
Under the creative direction of Alessandro Michele, Gucci has launched collections that openly celebrate diversity and self-expression, blurring traditional gender lines in fashion. Unisex pieces and designs that challenge gender norms have become emblematic of the new Gucci era, embodying an inclusive and progressive vision of fashion.

Support for LGBT+ causes
Beyond the fashion shows, Gucci has undertaken concrete initiatives in favor of LGBT+ rights. The brand supported in particular the "Chime for Change" project to finance campaigns and organizations dedicated to gender equality and the empowerment of women and LGBT+ people. Additionally, Gucci has made significant donations to anti-bullying campaigns, such as "Be a Star," which combats bullying in schools, including that experienced by LGBT+ youth.

Collaborations with LGBT+ icons

Gucci does not hesitate to highlight LGBT+ personalities in its advertising campaigns and artistic projects. Stars such as Jared Leto and Harry Styles, known for their androgynous style and support for the LGBT+ community, have been the faces of Gucci campaigns, spreading a message of diversity and acceptance. The collaboration with photographer Mick Rock for the "Gucci Guilty" project, starring Jared Leto, is an example of how Gucci uses its platform to openly celebrate and support the diversity of sexual identities and orientations.

A voice in pop culture

Gucci transcends fashion to become an influential voice in pop culture, using its notoriety to shine a light on LGBT+ issues and inspire positive change. By collaborating with films, musicians and artists who share its values of inclusion and diversity, Gucci amplifies the dialogue on LGBT+ rights and visibility, contributing to a more tolerant and open society.

Gucci's commitment to the LGBT+ community is a model of inclusion and support in the luxury sector. Combining creativity, fashion and activism, Gucci demonstrates that luxury is not just about beauty and elegance, but also about values, humanity and solidarity.

36

Gucci Beauty: By launching its beauty line, Gucci has expanded its influence beyond fashion, offering makeup products and fragrances that embody the brand's vision of style and elegance.

THE BEAUTY OF GUCCI

gucci.com

37

Participation in major fashion events: Gucci plays a central role in Milan fashion weeks and other fashion capitals, where its shows are among the most anticipated and influential, underlining its status as a leader in the fashion industry.

©Getty Images

38

Contribution to music: Gucci has forged close ties with the music industry, dressing musicians and celebrities for major events and initiating collaborations with artists, extending its cultural influence far beyond fashion.

39

Design Innovations: The brand has been a pioneer in introducing innovative fabrics and techniques, such as the use of Guccissima rubber, an exclusive material marked with the GG logo, used for shoes and accessories.

40

The Flora Scarf: Created in 1966 for Grace Kelly, the Flora scarf has become an iconic Gucci design, representing its commitment to elegance and femininity, with its detailed floral pattern continuing to inspire new collections.

Flora scarf by Gucci

The Flora scarf, designed by Gucci in 1966, embodies the very essence of elegance and femininity that characterize the brand. Born from a special order for Grace Kelly, this scarf quickly transcends its status as a simple accessory to become an iconic symbol of Gucci, perfectly illustrating the know-how and creativity of the Italian house.

A legendary creation

The story of the Flora scarf begins when Grace Kelly, accompanied by her husband, Prince Ranieri of Monaco, visits the Gucci boutique in Milan. Rodolfo Gucci, wanting to give the princess a unique gift, gives her a scarf specially designed for her. The Flora motif, with its delicately drawn flowers and insects, is a true work of textile art, reflecting Gucci's admiration for natural beauty and sophistication.

A timeless model

The design of the Flora scarf is notable for its complexity and symbolic richness. Representing more than ninety species of flowers, plants and insects, this motif is a paean to the diversity and beauty of nature. Beyond its aesthetic significance, it also evokes femininity in all its splendor, celebrating grace and delicacy through every detail.

A continuous source of inspiration

Over the years, the Flora motif has become a constant source of inspiration for new Gucci collections, appearing on various products from handbags to bags.

hand to clothing, including shoes and jewelry. Each reinterpretation of the Flora motif by Gucci's various creative directors has allowed it to be reinvented while preserving its original essence.

A lasting legacy

The Flora scarf is more than just a fashion accessory; it's a legacy, a testament to the unshakable bond between Gucci and style icons like Grace Kelly. Its enduring popularity among fashion lovers around the world is testament to its status as a classic piece, symbolizing Gucci's commitment to elegance, femininity and exceptional craftsmanship.

The Gucci Flora scarf remains an iconic piece of the house, a treasure of fashion history that continues to inspire and enchant, symbolizing the perfect union between art, nature and femininity.

41

The artistic evolution under **Alessandro Michele** Under the creative direction of Alessandro Michele since 2015, Gucci logos and symbols have undergone an artistic reinterpretation, blending the brand's rich history with a contemporary sensibility. Michele introduced new elements, such as bees, stars and floral motifs, which, while deviating from traditional logos, have become recognizable symbols of the new Gucci era.

Gucci logos: symbols of a luxury heritage
Since its founding in 1921 by Guccio Gucci in Florence, Italy, Gucci has established itself as one of the most iconic luxury brands in the world.

The Double G: Gucci's most iconic logo, the interlocking double G, pays homage to the brand's founder, Guccio Gucci. Introduced in the 1960s, this logo has become synonymous with luxury and style, representing both tradition and modernity. The two consecutive Gs are a hymn to Italian excellence and craftsmanship, values that Gucci has always supported.

The Web Stripe: While technically not a logo, the green-red-green Web Stripe is immediately associated with Gucci. Inspired by the straps of equestrian saddles, this tricolor stripe symbolizes the origin of the brand and its connection with the equestrian world. It has become an iconic design element, appearing on a multitude of products, from bags and shoes to clothing.

The horse's bit: Another distinctive symbol of Gucci is the horse's bit, also inspired by the brand's equestrian tradition. First used in the 1950s, the horse bit recalls Guccio Gucci's original inspiration and has become a recurring motif, embodying luxury and sophistication.

The Diamante Pattern The Diamante pattern, with its unique design of small interlocking diamonds, is one of Gucci's oldest motifs, dating back to the 1930s. Although less visible today, this motif remains an important part of Gucci's history, symbolizing attention to detail and timeless quality.

42

Gucci Museum: Located in Florence, the Gucci Museum celebrates the history of the brand through exhibitions of archives, artworks and iconic pieces, offering a glimpse of its evolution since its founding.

43

Influence on street fashion: Gucci has embraced and influenced street fashion, with pieces that have become must-haves for fashionistas and influencers, marking the fusion between luxury and casual chic.

REVOLUTION IN LUXURY FASHION

Gucci bags are not just accessories; they are the symbol of a rich history of Italian luxury, innovation and craftsmanship.

Since the brand was founded by Guccio Gucci in 1921, Gucci bags have evolved to become iconic pieces of global fashion, embodying the timeless elegance and style associated with the Italian fashion house.

Each Gucci bag tells a story, a fusion of tradition, creativity and meticulous attention to detail.

The Bamboo bag, for example, was born in the 1940s in response to shortages of traditional materials, illustrating Gucci's ingenuity in tackling challenges.

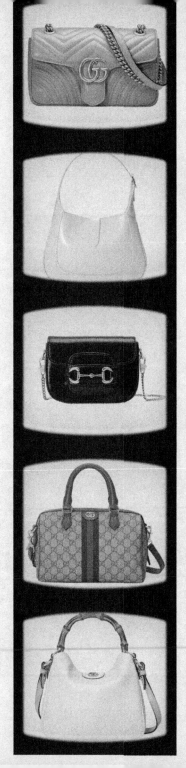

Capsule Collection 100: To celebrate its centenary in 2021, Gucci has launched a special capsule collection that revisits the brand's archives, showcasing its evolution over the century and its impact on contemporary fashion.

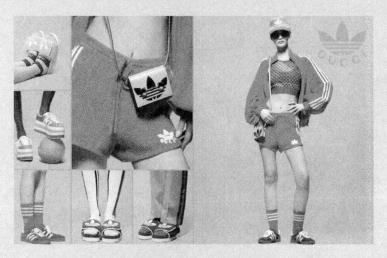

The capsule collection is revealed in a very sporty campaign.

gucci.com

The Gucci Equilibrium Platform: This initiative aims to promote transparency and social and environmental action, focusing on creating a more sustainable and just future, demonstrating Gucci's commitment to having a positive impact on the world.

46

The "Gucci Places" project: Gucci launched
the "Gucci Places" project to celebrate and
share the places around the world that inspire
the brand, from historic boutiques to secret
gardens, highlighting their beauty and
uniqueness.

Gucci Places: Journey to the heart of the luxury maison's inspirations

The "Gucci Places" project embodies Gucci's spirit of wanderlust and insatiable curiosity, inviting visitors to explore unique places around the world that have captured the essence and inspired the brand's universe. From iconic boutiques to the most secret corners, each "Gucci Place" is a window into the history, culture and elegance that fuel Gucci's creativity.

A passport to inspiration

Launched with the idea of creating a dialogue between the brand's admirers and its geographical sources of inspiration, "Gucci Places" celebrates the hidden beauty and stories behind often unexpected places. Whether it's an ancient castle, a lush botanical garden or a historic boutique, each selected location shares an affinity with Gucci's aesthetic and values.

The magic of Chatsworth

House Among the selected "Gucci Places", Chatsworth House in the United Kingdom has a particularly fascinating history. This majestic residence, rich in art and history, was the setting for Gucci's Cruise 2017 campaign. But beyond its captivating aesthetic, Chatsworth House has created a unique connection with Gucci thanks to the Duchess of Devonshire, Deborah Cavendish, a figure of style and elegance recognized for her love of Gucci jewellery. This partnership between Gucci and Chatsworth House perfectly illustrates how "Gucci Places" are not chosen just for them beauty, but for the deep and personal resonances they share with the brand.

More than just a visit
"Gucci Places" aims to encourage people to discover these places for themselves, experience their unique atmosphere and understand why they have become a source of inspiration for Gucci. To enrich the experience, Gucci offers a dedicated app, which offers detailed stories about each location, as well as exclusive collectible badges for those who visit, turning each exploration into a true luxury treasure hunt.

A celebration of cultural diversity
Through "Gucci Places", Gucci not only celebrates geographical and cultural diversity, but also highlights the importance of preserving heritage and promoting the arts in all their forms. This project demonstrates Gucci's vision: a brand that transcends fashion to embrace the richness of our world, creating bridges between eras, cultures and passions.

"Gucci Places" is not just an invitation to travel; is an invitation to explore the world through the eyes of Gucci, in search of beauty, history and inspiration. This is further proof that Gucci, in addition to being a luxury house, is a true teller of universal stories, weaving indelible links between past, present and future.

47

Snoop Dogg, a hip-hop icon known for his unique and extravagant style, was often seen wearing Gucci clothing, marking the union between the worlds of music and high fashion. His affection for Gucci highlights how the brand transcends cultural boundaries, becoming a symbol of luxury and style in the world of rap.

48

Ryan Gosling, an actor with undeniable charisma, was chosen as the face of the new Gucci perfume campaign, elegantly embodying the contemporary and timeless spirit of the brand. His collaboration with Gucci, combining classic charm and modernity, reveals how the luxury house constantly seeks to blend its heritage with figures that reflect a new generation sophistication.

The Gucci Muses: ambassadors of reinvented luxury
Over the decades, Gucci has surrounded himself with charismatic muses, embodying the spirit and values of the brand. These ambassadors, hailing from the worlds of film, music, fashion and even activism, don't just represent Gucci; they actively participate in the redefinition of luxury and the affirmation of the unique identity of the brand. Each muse brings with it its own history, its own style and its own vision, thus enriching the Gucci world.

From timeless icons to new faces, from Jane Birkin to Harry Styles, via Florence Welch and Jared Leto, Gucci's muses form an eclectic pantheon of influential personalities. These collaborations perfectly illustrate Gucci's ability to navigate between tradition and modernity, choosing ambassadors who reflect both the brand's heritage and its direction into the future.

Miley Cyrus and the spirit of rebellion: Miley Cyrus, with her rebellious spirit and her commitment to diversity and inclusion, perfectly represents the new wave of Gucci muses. Her collaboration with the brand, particularly for the Gucci Flora perfume, captures the essence of bold and independent femininity, in perfect harmony with Alessandro Michele's vision.

Harry Styles: A symbol of fluidity: Harry Styles, known for his androgynous style and music, embodies Gucci's unconventional approach to fashion. His ability to blur the lines between genres and embrace a unique aesthetic makes him an iconic figure for the brand, reflecting the spirit of openness and freedom that characterizes Gucci under Michele's leadership.

Jared Leto: The Art of Metamorphosis: Jared Leto, with his chameleonic screen and stage presence, as well as his commitment to ecological and social causes, is a living embodiment of Gucci values. His friendship with Alessandro Michele and his important Gucci appearances on red carpets around the world testify to the alchemy between his personality and the brand's identity.

49

Miley Cyrus, with her bold personality and chameleon-like style, was the face of Gucci's "Flora" fragrance, capturing the essence of freedom and femininity that characterizes the brand. His participation in this campaign is not limited to his image; embodies Gucci's commitment to individual expression and diversity, highlighting how the brand embraces and celebrates unique voices in the world of fashion and beyond.

Miley Cyrus, the American pop icon known for her boldness, free spirit and commitment to social causes, has become an iconic muse for Gucci, perfectly embodying the spirit of the brand under the creative direction of Alessandro Michele. The collaboration between Miley Cyrus and Gucci marks a fusion of two worlds, that of vibrant pop culture and that of timeless luxury, illustrating the brand's desire to associate itself with personalities that reflect its values of individuality, expression of self-esteem and support of community LGBTQ· rights and diversity.

——— GUCCI

50

Jared Leto, with his eclectic style and bold approach to fashion, has become an iconic ambassador for Gucci, as well as being the face of the Gucci Guilty fragrance line. His close relationship with Alessandro Michele, the brand's creative director, and his extraordinary appearances in Gucci on red carpets highlight a perfect synergy between the actor and the house, illustrating how Gucci celebrates personalities who push the boundaries of creativity and self-determination. expression.

51

Tapis rouge Influence: Gucci designs are a favorite choice of celebrities at red carpet events, where the brand is regularly highlighted for its unique blend of contemporary glamor and classic sophistication.

Dakota Johnson wears a Gucci party girl dress on the red carpet | French Vogue

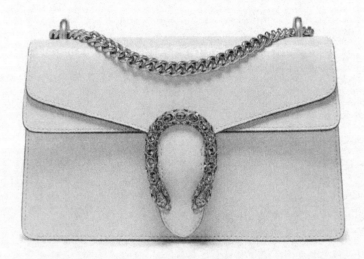

52

The Dionysus Bag: Introduced in 2015, the Dionysus bag has quickly become one of Gucci's most desirable bags, famous for its tiger head-shaped clasp, symbolizing Greek mythology and the history of the brand.

53

Launch of Gucci Circular Lines: As part of its commitment to sustainability, Gucci introduced Gucci Circular Lines, an initiative designed to promote circularity. This includes creating collections with recycled, regenerated and bio-based materials, in order to minimize environmental impact.

GUCCI

Commitment to Contemporary Art: Through collaborations with contemporary artists and support of art exhibitions around the world, Gucci shows its commitment to contemporary art and its desire to break the boundaries between fashion and art.

54

ILLEGAL'
BUSINESS

55

Gucci has always been at the forefront of innovation in the world of fashion, but its commitment to contemporary art reveals an additional dimension of the brand, that of a bold bridge between luxury and artistic expression. By collaborating with contemporary artists and supporting art exhibitions around the world, Gucci transcends traditional boundaries, affirming that fashion is not just about clothes but also an art form in its own right.

Illegalartbusiness Mickey Gucci It's raining, 2020

Mixed media (acrylic and aerosol) on canvas Signed
lower right Unique work Framed

100 x 80 cm

Dimensions:
- Height: 100cm
- Width: 80 cm

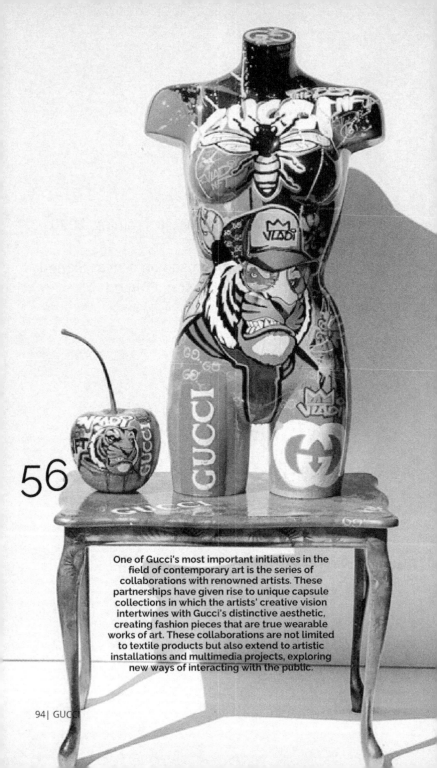

56

One of Gucci's most important initiatives in the field of contemporary art is the series of collaborations with renowned artists. These partnerships have given rise to unique capsule collections in which the artists' creative vision intertwines with Gucci's distinctive aesthetic, creating fashion pieces that are true wearable works of art. These collaborations are not limited to textile products but also extend to artistic installations and multimedia projects, exploring new ways of interacting with the public.

Place of work: France

Unique sculpture by Art VLADI 1/1 2022 with certificate of authenticity and protection with Gucci-style automotive paint. Art VLADI is the artist who created sculptures, paintings and jackets for Floyd Mayweather and Jordan Belfort 'The Wolf of Wallstreet'.
Seller information

Professional art gallery • France

GUCCI
BLOOM

Gucci flourishes

GUCCI FASHION
THE SCENT

Launched in 2017, Gucci Bloom is the olfactory expression of the essence of a garden in full bloom, a creation that marks a turning point in the world of perfumes from the famous Italian luxury house. Designed under the creative direction of Alessandro Michele, this fragrance is a true celebration of femininity, authenticity and vitality. Gucci Bloom embodies Michele's vision for a modern woman who lives in harmony with her inner nature, freely exploring and expressing her identity.

GUCCI

Gucci Boutique: more than just shops, immersive experiences

Gucci boutiques are not just points of sale; they reflect the complex and rich universe of the brand, offering visitors much more than a traditional shopping experience. Each Gucci store is designed to immerse customers in the brand's aesthetic and philosophy, blending historical heritage, contemporary luxury and artistic innovation. Walking through the doors of a Gucci boutique, customers enter a world where fashion meets art, culture and design.

A unique architectural design: the interior design of the Gucci boutiques is the result of a close collaboration between the best architects and the creative director of the brand, Alessandro Michele. The interior design pays homage to Italian elegance and sophistication by incorporating contemporary and eclectic elements. From the marble floors and rich tapestries to the antique furniture and modern art installations, every detail contributes to creating a luxurious and welcoming atmosphere.

Iconic locations: Gucci boutiques are located in some of the most prestigious streets and luxurious neighborhoods in the world, from Via Montenapoleone in Milan to 5th Avenue in New York, to Faubourg Saint-Honoré in Paris. These strategic positions underline the brand's status in the world of luxury and facilitate access to a demanding international clientele.

Personalized customer experience: Gucci places customer experience at the center of its retail strategy. The boutiques offer a high level of personalized service, with expert sales consultants who guide customers through the collections and help them find pieces that reflect their personal style. Some stores also offer customization services, allowing customers to create one-of-a-kind pieces.

57

Innovation and Technology: In addition to aesthetics and service, Gucci integrates innovation and technology into its stores to enhance the shopping experience. This includes the use of augmented reality to virtually try on accessories, interactive screens showing collection stories, and mobile apps for a seamless shopping experience.

58

Commitment to Sustainability: In line with its commitment to sustainability, Gucci works to reduce the environmental impact of its stores. This involves the use of sustainable materials in construction and interior design, as well as the adoption of eco-responsible practices in the daily management of the stores.

59

Gucci made history by including Ellie Goldstein, a model with Down syndrome, in its 2020 beauty campaign, breaking traditional fashion barriers and celebrating diversity in all its forms. This initiative highlights Gucci's commitment to promoting inclusion and redefining beauty standards in the fashion industry.

60

The Gucci Manifesto: The "Gucci Manifesto" collection highlights masks as a symbol of freedom of expression, reflecting Alessandro Michele's unique and sometimes subversive aesthetic and underlining the brand's message of individuality and self-expression.

61

Gucci Fest: Gucci broke new ground by launching "Gucci Fest," an online fashion and film festival, showcasing its new collection and short films from emerging designers, demonstrating its commitment to new storytelling platforms.

Gucci: at the crossroads between innovation and modernity

Gucci, a timeless symbol of luxury, has constantly reinvented itself by embracing innovation and modernity, while remaining true to its rich heritage. Under the creative direction of Alessandro Michele, the brand has redefined the codes of fashion by fusing the past with avant-garde elements, demonstrating that tradition and innovation can coexist harmoniously.

The adoption of digital technologies illustrates Gucci's commitment to innovation. The brand pioneered the use of augmented reality to virtually try on products, offering an engaging and interactive shopping experience to a global customer base. Additionally, Gucci has explored the metaverse and digital products, establishing its position at the forefront of digital luxury.

Gucci has also stood out for its commitment to sustainability and social responsibility. By eliminating fur and launching Gucci Circular Lines, the brand has taken significant steps towards reducing its environmental impact, proving that luxury can be both ethical and eco-friendly.

Innovative collaborations with artists, musicians and streetwear brands have allowed Gucci to reach a diverse audience and remain relevant in contemporary culture. These partnerships, at the intersection of fashion, art and music, highlight Gucci's ability to break traditional boundaries and set new trends.

Gucci embodies the spirit of innovation and modernity, demonstrating that a historic brand can not only adapt to the developments of its time but also anticipate them. Gucci continues to shape the future of fashion with courage, creativity and awareness, redefining luxury for the new era.

62

Gucci in space: In 2017, Gucci sent some of its designs into space as part of a project with the Italian Space Agency, literally symbolizing the brand's ambition to push the boundaries of what's possible.

time

Gucci Italia photo shoot

63

The "So Deer To Me" project: Gucci presented a campaign committed to the preservation of flora and fauna, illustrating its commitment to protecting biodiversity and promoting a sustainable future for the planet.

64

Commitment to Italian craftsmanship: By highlighting Italian craftsmanship through its collections, Gucci celebrates traditional skills and the excellence of Italian know-how, thus supporting the local economy and preserving precious cultural heritage.

With these actions and commitments, Gucci continues to write its history, not only as an iconic fashion house but also as a leader in the transformation towards a more conscious and responsible fashion industry. Gucci's extraordinary journey, characterized by innovation, creativity and a deep commitment to social and environmental values, is a source of inspiration, demonstrating that luxury and responsibility can coexist harmoniously.

Printed in Great Britain
by Amazon